to

from

For Daisy, Elliot and Tom, with love A.A.

Text by Lois Rock

A Lion Children's Book
an imprint of
Lion Hudson plc
Wilkinson House, Jordan Hill Road,
Oxford OX2 8DR, England
www.lionhudson.com
ISBN 978 0 7459 6911 4

First edition 2009
This printing July 2009
1 3 5 7 9 10 8 6 4 2 0

A catalogue record for this book is available
from the British Library

Typeset in 15/21 Baskerville
Printed and bound in China by Printplus Ltd

my very first

Nativity Story

Words by
Lois Rock

Pictures by
Alex Ayliffe

LION CHILDREN'S

The flowers bobbed and curtsied as the angel Gabriel passed by.

“Nazareth looks lovely in the spring,” said Gabriel, “but I have work to do. I need to give Mary a message from God.

“I can see her over there.”

Mary was startled to see the angel.

“Don’t be afraid,” said Gabriel. “God has chosen you to be the mother of a very special baby – Jesus.”

The news puzzled Mary.

“I can’t be a mother,” she answered. “I’m not Joseph’s wife yet.”

“The baby will be God’s son,” replied Gabriel. “Everything will happen because of God.”

“Oh,” said Mary. “I will always do what God wants.”

Joseph soon heard the news about Mary.

"She's going to have a baby – but it's not mine," he wept.

"I really want to marry her – but is that still the right thing to do?"

In a dream, an angel spoke to him.

"Of course you must marry Mary. God has chosen you to look after her and the baby."

Joseph woke up feeling happy again.

Then more news arrived – news for everyone.

“The emperor has made a new law,” said the messenger. “All of you must go to your home towns and put your names on a big list.”

“Why?” asked the people of Nazareth.

"It's to check you're all paying your tax money," said the messenger glumly.

Joseph went to speak to Mary.

"You must come with me to Bethlehem," he said. "We shall be on the list as husband and wife."

Joseph and Mary plodded down the long road to Bethlehem.

Because of the emperor's new law, lots of people were going to their home towns.

When Mary and Joseph reached Bethlehem, there was no room left in the inn.

"My baby is going to be born very soon," whispered Mary. "We need somewhere to stay for the night."

At last, they found shelter in a stable.

“It’s not a proper room,” said Joseph, “but it’s all we have. I hope the animals don’t bother you.”

There, in the stable, Mary's baby was born.

She wrapped him in swaddling clothes to keep him snug and warm.

"This feeding trough is a bit like a cradle," said Joseph. "I can make it cosy for the baby."

"It's perfect," said Mary, as she laid baby Jesus in the manger.

Soon it was night-time in Bethlehem. Out on the hillside, shepherds were guarding their sheep.

"We need to keep them safe from foxes," said one.

"And jackals," said another.

"And wolves and bears and lions," said the little shepherd boy. "I'm not afraid of anything."

Suddenly a light flashed through the sky, brighter than lightning.

The shepherds hugged each other in fright.

The shepherd boy hid behind a sheep.

Then they saw the angel.

"Don't be afraid," said the angel. "I have good news. Tonight, in Bethlehem, God's son has been born.

"He will be greater than the greatest king.

"He will bring joy to all the world.

"Tonight, in Bethlehem, he is cradled in a manger."

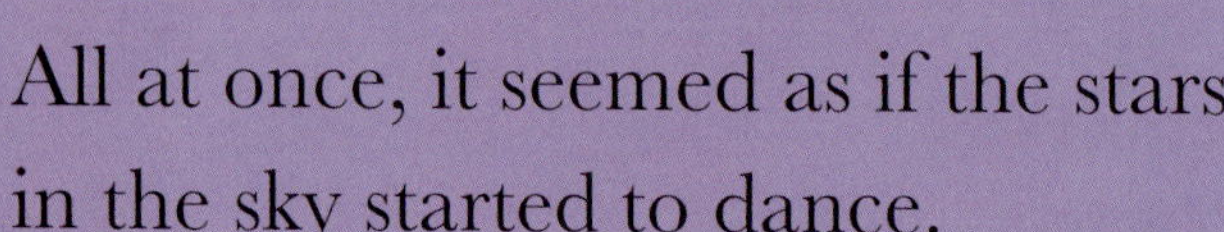

All at once, it seemed as if the stars in the sky started to dance.

In their glittering light, a choir of angels sang joyful songs.

"Glory to God in heaven!"

"Peace to everyone on earth!"

The shepherds gazed in wonder.

When the songs were sung, the night was once again still and silent.

“Let’s go to Bethlehem,” whispered the shepherd boy. “I want to know if the message is true…or if I’ve just been dreaming.”

Off they all went to the little town on the hilltop.

Everywhere, they listened hard. They were hoping to hear the gentle cry of a newborn baby.

At last they found the place. Joseph and Mary and baby Jesus were there.

The little shepherd boy suddenly felt shy. Mary smiled. “Come closer,” she said.

He tiptoed nearer and touched the baby’s hand. The tiny fingers gripped him tight.

"Now tell me everything about the angels," said Mary. "I want to know exactly what they said."

When the telling was done, the shepherds set off, back to the hillside.

Mary held her baby as she watched them step out into the dark night.

The shepherd boy turned back to wave.

It seemed, for a moment, as if he were looking right into heaven.

He felt that he would never be afraid ever again.

Long before and far away, three men looked up at the night sky. The star shone back at them, clear and bright.

“I think it is a messenger star,” said one.

“I think I understand the message,” said the second. “A new king has been born.”

“Then we should go and look for him,” said the third.

They all agreed that this was the wise thing to do.

They set off on their journey. The star lit their way over hills and valleys, mile after mile.

At last they came to the city of Jerusalem.

“We are looking for a newborn king,” they told the townspeople. “Is he here?”

No one knew anything about a new baby king but the news of the travellers spread quickly.

Inside the palace, King Herod was puzzled.

“Can anyone explain what’s going on?” he growled.

The priests came with their precious books.

“Listen to what’s written here: God will send a special king one day. He will be born in Bethlehem.”

Herod sent for the wise men.

“Try to find the king in Bethlehem,” he said. “I, too, want to see him.”

He watched the men go, then muttered, “I want to get rid of this king.”

The wise men went
along the road
to Bethlehem.

The star lit the way.

It hung low over a little house in the town.

Inside, the wise men found Mary and her little boy, Jesus.

The men bowed to show their respect.

“I bring a gift of gold,” said one, “for the king who will be rich beyond all telling.”

“I bring frankincense,” said the second.

“Like a priest, this king will help people be friends with God.”

“I bring myrrh,” said the third. “It is ointment that heals. This king will be able to heal everyone and everything.”

After the gift-giving, the men whispered together, "Let's not go back to Herod. It feels wrong to tell him about this wonderful king."

They went home by a different road.

In a dream, an angel spoke to Joseph.

"Hurry. There is danger. Take Mary and Jesus far away from here."

And so they went, trusting in
God's love and care for always.

Away in a manger, no crib for a bed,
The little Lord Jesus laid down his sweet head.
The stars in the bright sky looked down
where he lay,
The little Lord Jesus asleep on the hay.

The cattle are lowing, the baby awakes,
But little Lord Jesus, no crying he makes.
I love thee, Lord Jesus! Look down from the sky,
And stay by my side until morning is nigh.

Be near me, Lord Jesus, I ask thee to stay
Close by me for ever, and love me, I pray.
Bless all the dear children in thy tender care,
And fit us for heaven, to live with thee there.

A traditional Christmas carol